BOOK 2

HAL LEONARD
GUITAR METHOD

GUITAR FOR KIDS

A Beginner's Guide with
Step-by-Step Instruction for
Acoustic and Electric Guitar

BY CHAD JOHNSON

To access audio, visit:
www.halleonard.com/mylibrary

Enter Code
7754-1118-9188-2172

ISBN 978-1-4803-9261-8

Visit Hal Leonard Online at
www.halleonard.com

World headquarters, contact:
Hal Leonard
7777 West Bluemound Road
Milwaukee, WI 53213
Email: info@halleonard.com

In Europe, contact:
Hal Leonard Europe Limited
1 Red Place
London, W1K 6PL
Email: info@halleonardeurope.com

In Australia, contact:
Hal Leonard Australia Pty. Ltd.
4 Lentara Court
Cheltenham, Victoria, 3192 Australia
Email: info@halleonard.com.au

THE E CHORD

The E chord is a favorite of guitarists everywhere. You'll press three notes at the same time. Strum through all six strings.

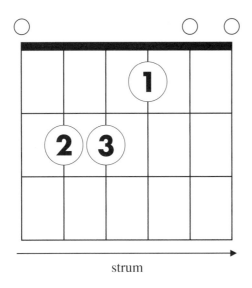

strum

Strum the chord in the rhythm shown below for this next song. Remember that the **half rest** means to be silent for two beats, and the **whole rest** means to be silent for the whole measure (four beats).

E CHORD ROCK

TEACHER MELODY:

You remember your A and D chords from the last book, right? Play them along with the new E chord on this next song. Play the repeated verse section three times.

BLOWIN' IN THE WIND 🔊

Words and Music
by Bob Dylan

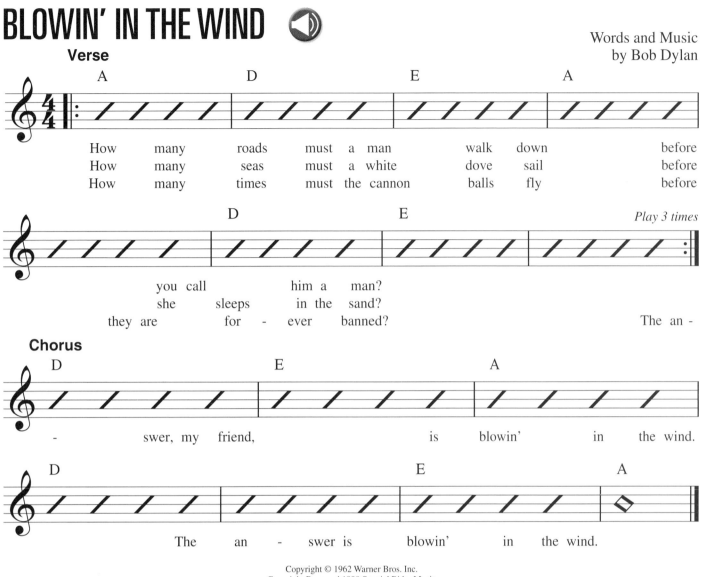

Verse

How many roads must a man walk down before
How many seas must a white dove sail before
How many times must the cannon balls fly before

Play 3 times

you call him a man?
she sleeps in the sand?
they are for - ever banned? The an -

Chorus

- swer, my friend, is blowin' in the wind.

The an - swer is blowin' in the wind.

TEACHER MELODY:

THE A MINOR CHORD

You'll use three fingers for this chord as well. It looks very similar to the E chord, only your fingers all move over one string. Strum strings 5–1.

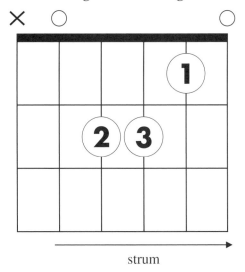

strum

A HORSE WITH NO NAME

Words and Music
by Dewey Bunnell

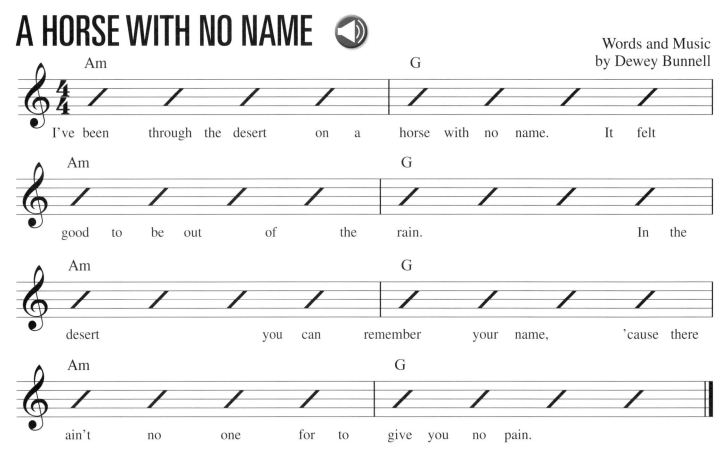

Am	G
I've been through the desert on a horse with no name. It felt

Am	G
good to be out of the rain. In the

Am	G
desert you can remember your name, 'cause there

Am	G
ain't no one for to give you no pain.

TEACHER MELODY:

In this next song, you'll use your new Am and E chords together.

FEVER

Words and Music
by John Davenport and Eddie Cooley

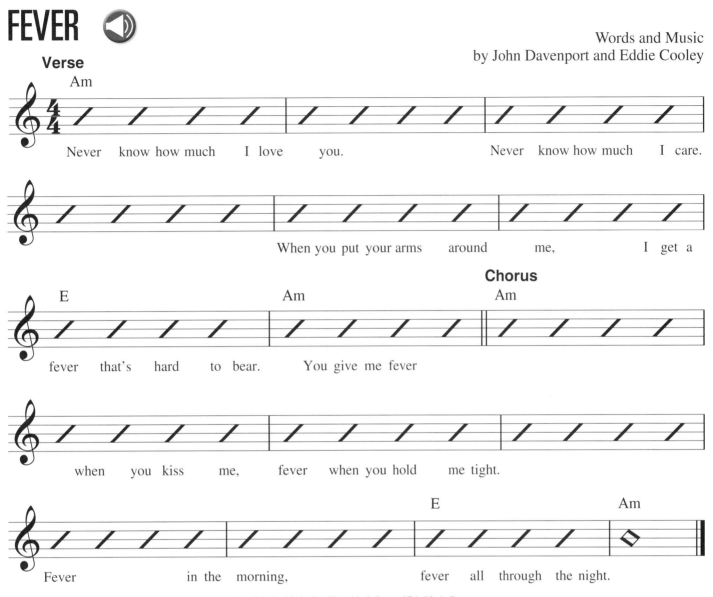

TEACHER MELODY:

THE FULL C & G CHORDS

You learned a small version of the C chord in Book 1 that used only three strings. Now let's look at the full version, which contains five strings.

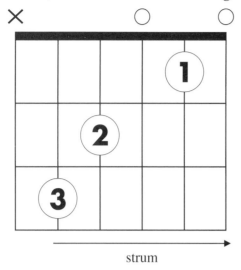

strum

Now let's learn a full, six-string version of a G chord.

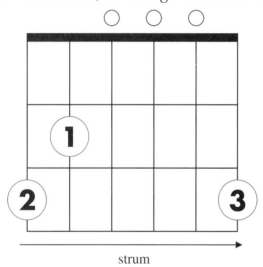

strum

KNOCKIN' ON HEAVEN'S DOOR

Words and Music
by Bob Dylan

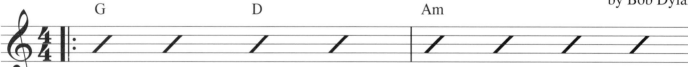

| G | D | Am |

Knock, knock, knocking on Heaven's door.

| G | D | C | G |

Knock, knock, knocking on Heaven's door.

TEACHER MELODY:

THE FULL E MINOR CHORD

And here's the full, six-string version of the Em chord you learned in Book 1.

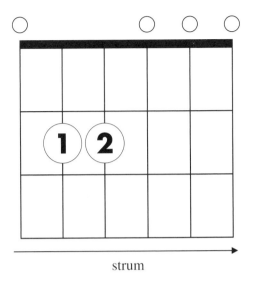

strum

CHORD TO CHORD

You now know how to play two new chords and three new versions of others. Let's practice changing between two chords at a time. Start off slowly!

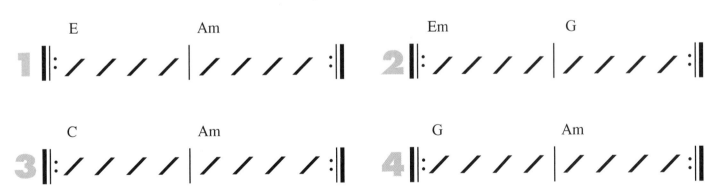

At the end of Book 1, you learned how to strum twice for each beat, using downstrums and upstrums. Try that for this next song. The **first and second endings** tell you to play the measure with the "1" bracket the first time through. When you repeat, skip over the "1" measure to the one marked "2" for the ending.

FIELDS OF GOLD

Music and Lyrics by Sting

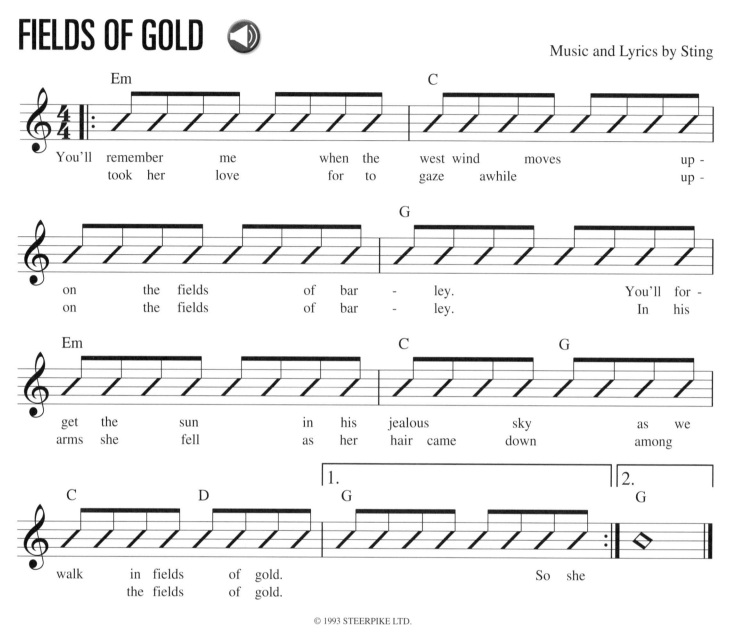

You'll remember me when the west wind moves up -
took her love for to gaze awhile up -

on the fields of bar - ley. You'll for -
on the fields of bar - ley. In his

get the sun in his jealous sky as we
arms she fell as her hair came down among

1.
walk in fields of gold.
the fields of gold.

2.
So she

TEACHER MELODY:

Many songs mix different patterns of downstrums and upstrums. In this next song, you'll strum down, down, down-up, down-up.

LET IT GO

from Disney's Animated Feature FROZEN
Music and Lyrics by
Kristen Anderson-Lopez and Robert Lopez

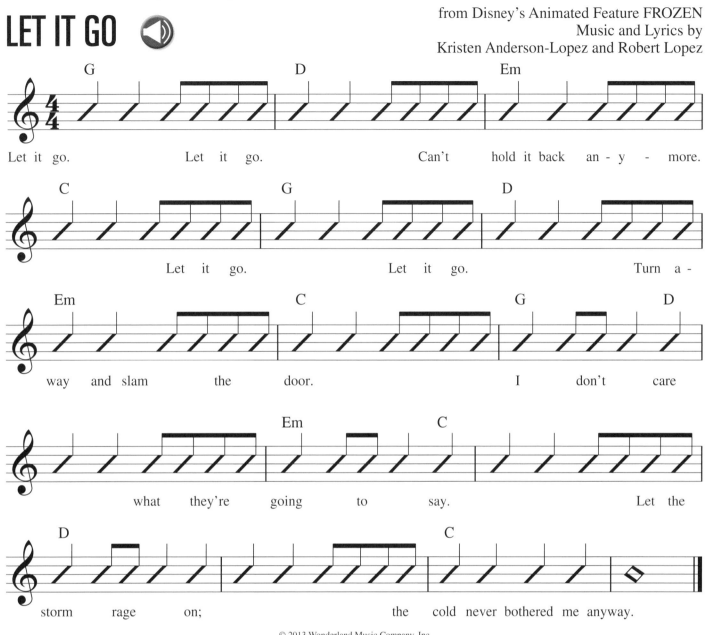

Let it go. Let it go. Can't hold it back an - y - more.

Let it go. Let it go. Turn a -

way and slam the door. I don't care

what they're going to say. Let the

storm rage on; the cold never bothered me anyway.

TEACHER MELODY:

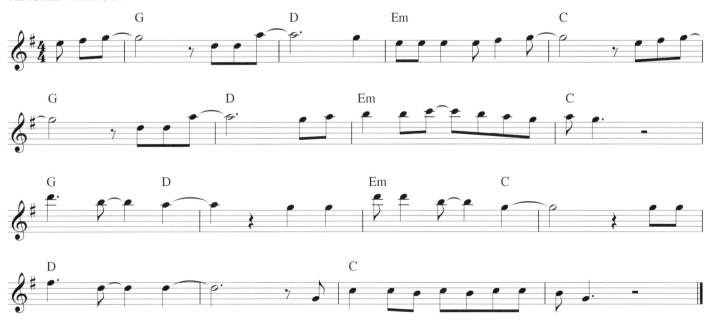

NOTE REVIEW

In Book 1, you learned notes on strings 3, 2, and 1. Before we learn notes on the rest of the strings, let's play a game to see if you can remember all the notes you've learned already.

For each grid, write the name of the note shown. Try to do it without peeking at Book 1 if you can! (Answers are on the bottom of the page.)

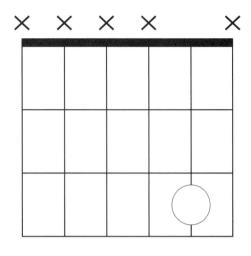

1. _____

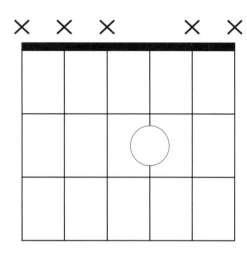

2. _____

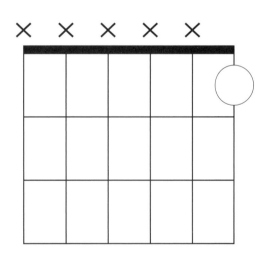

3. _____

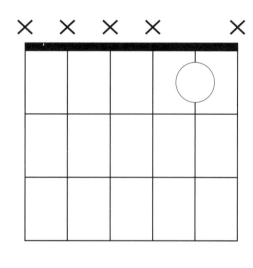

4. _____

5) What note is the open 1st string? _____

6) What note is the open 2nd string? _____

7) What note is the open 3rd string? _____

8) What's the note on fret 3 of the 1st string? _____

So how did you do?

10

CHORD REVIEW

And now let's review all the chords you learned in Book 1 while we're at it!

Name each chord below:

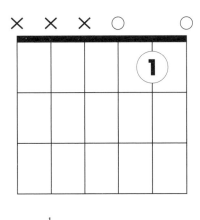

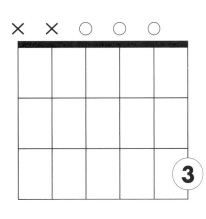

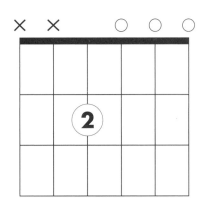

1. _____

2. _____

3. _____

These are a little harder. Complete each chord by drawing in the missing note on the string with the question mark.

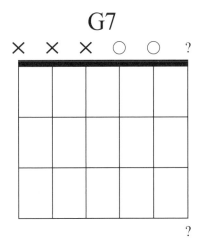

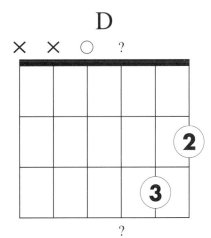

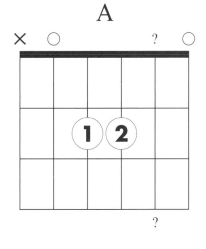

Answer Key:

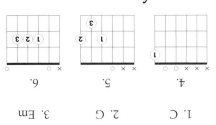

6.   5.   4.

1. C   2. G   3. Em

11

THE NOTE E

To play the lowest note available on your guitar, pluck the open 6th string using a downstroke.

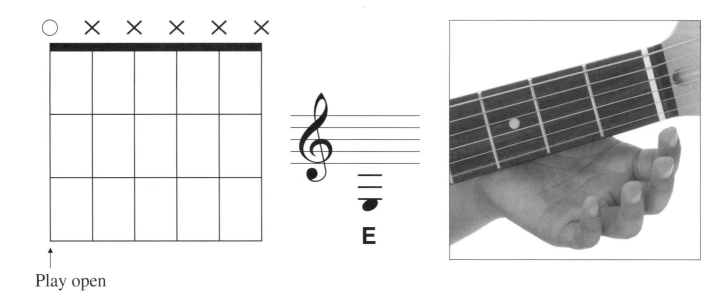

Play open

E

ONE-NOTE ROCK

TEACHER ACCOMPANIMENT:

A **tie** ⌣ combines two or more notes. A quarter note tied to a quarter note, for example, lasts for two beats, or the same as a half note.

FANCY ROCK — SUIT AND TIE REQUIRED

TEACHER ACCOMPANIMENT:

THE NOTE F

Use your 1st finger to press the 6th string at the 1st fret.

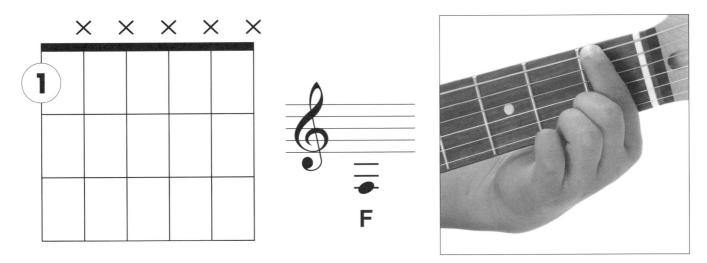

An **eighth note** ♪ lasts for half a beat. There are two eighth notes for every beat in a 4/4 or 3/4 time signature. When playing eighth notes, count them by saying, "one and two and three and four and."

SPANISH ROCK

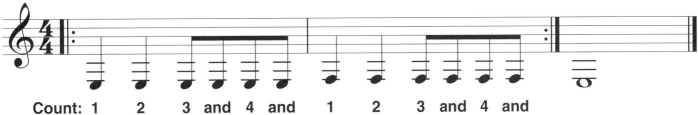

Count: 1   2   3 and 4 and   1   2   3 and 4 and

TEACHER ACCOMPANIMENT:

SHARK ATTACK

THE NOTE G

Use your 3rd finger to press the 6th string at the 3rd fret.

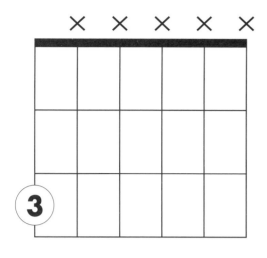

G

BLUES RIFF

TEACHER ACCOMPANIMENT:

TWO-NOTE GROOVE

TEACHER ACCOMPANIMENT:

THE NOTE A

Now let's move to the 5th string. To play a low A note, pluck the open 5th string.

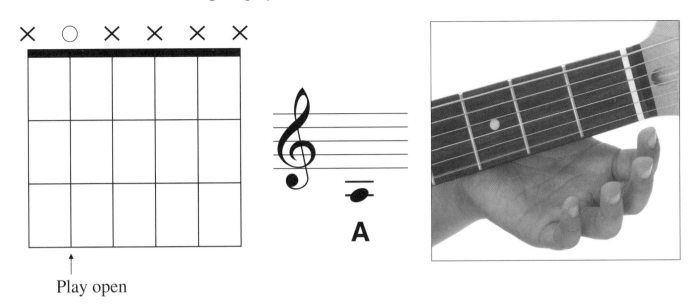

Play open

A

DRIVING ROCK

TEACHER ACCOMPANIMENT:

TAKE A WALK

TEACHER ACCOMPANIMENT:

THE NOTE B

Use your 2nd finger to press the 5th string at the 2nd fret.

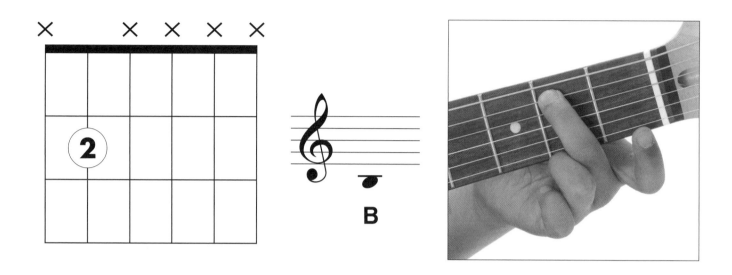

An **eighth rest** ⅞ means to be silent for half of a beat. Count along as you play the example below.

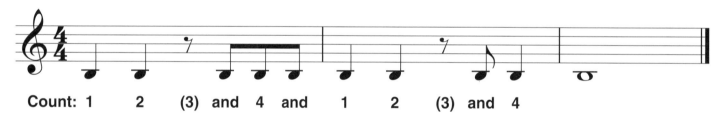

Count: 1   2   (3) and 4 and   1   2   (3) and 4

ROCK CLIMBING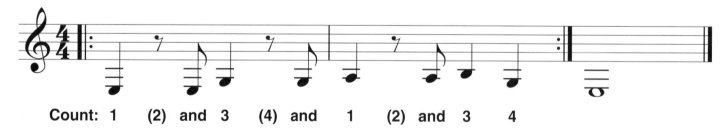

Count: 1   (2) and 3   (4) and   1   (2) and 3   4

TEACHER ACCOMPANIMENT:

let ring throughout

THE NOTE C

Use your 3rd finger to press the 5th string at the 3rd fret.

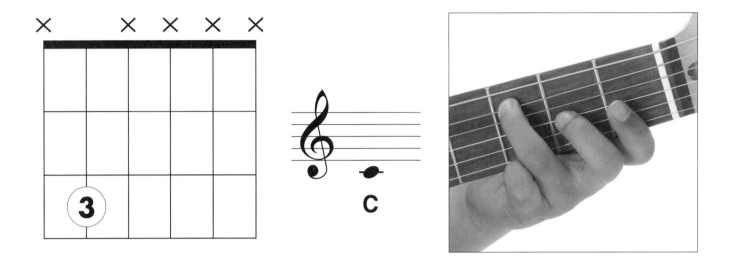

MOODY ROCK

TEACHER ACCOMPANIMENT:

NOTE REVIEW

You've learned six new notes now: three on the 6th string and three on the 5th string.

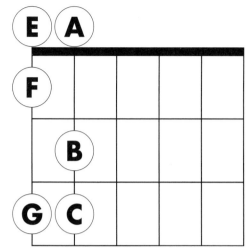

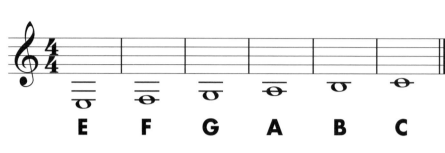

E   F   G   A   B   C

Did You Notice?

The notes on the low E (6th) string are the same as those on the high E (1st) string. The difference is that the notes on the 1st string are two **octaves** higher than the ones on the 6th.

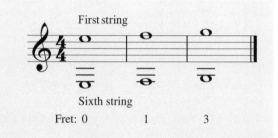

The notes in these exercises move from string to string. As you're playing one note, look ahead to the next and get your fingers in position.

1    **2**

3    **4**

BASS LINE RIFF 🔊

TEACHER ACCOMPANIMENT:

18

THE D7 CHORD

The D7 chord looks like the D chord, but the triangle shape points the other direction.

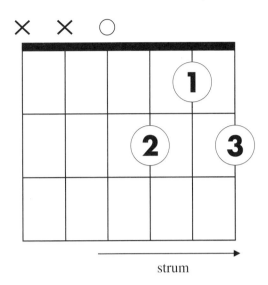

strum

Follow the written strum pattern in this next song that includes the D7 chord.

DEEP IN THE HEART OF TEXAS

Words by June Hershey
Music by Don Swander

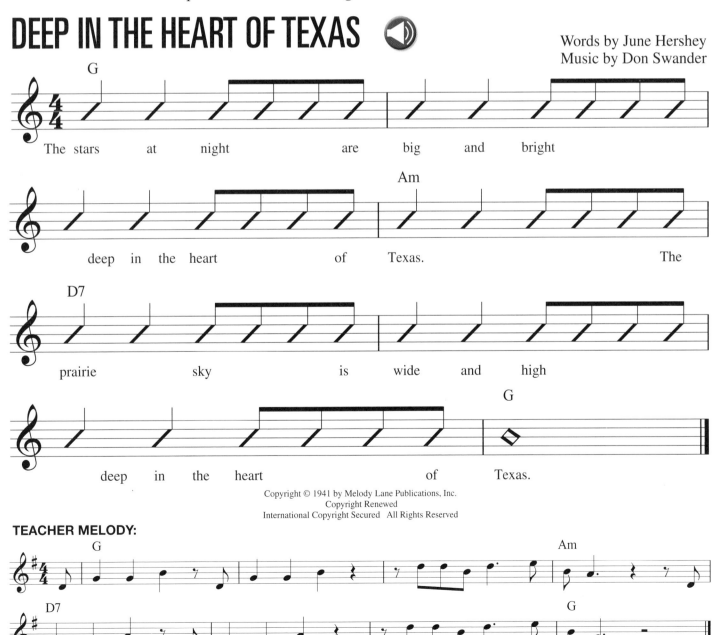

THE D MINOR CHORD

The D minor chord uses the same strings as D and D7, but it looks a bit different.

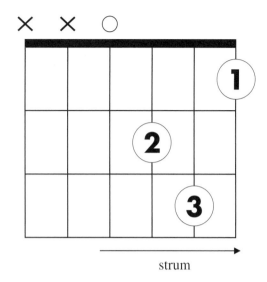

strum

In this song, you'll use Dm and D chords.

DUST IN THE WIND

Words and Music
by Kerry Livgren

Verse

| C | G | Am | G | Dm | Am |

I close my eyes — only for a moment and the moment's gone.
All my dreams — pass before my eyes, a curiosity.

Chorus

| D | G | Am | G | D | G | Am |

Dust in the wind. All we are is dust in the wind.

TEACHER MELODY:

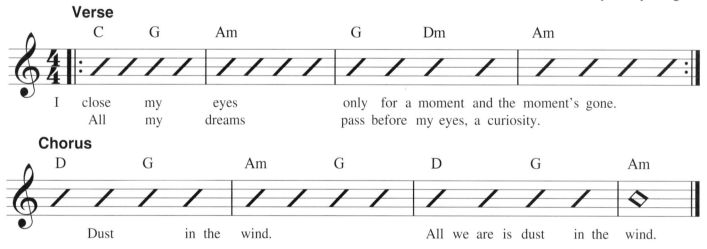

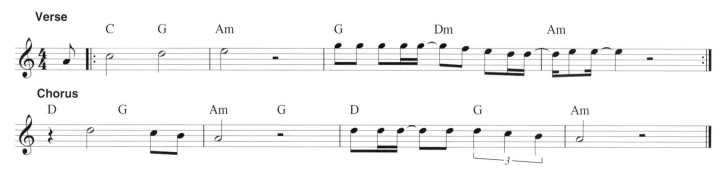

THE E7 & A7 CHORDS

If you know your E chord, then E7 is easy!

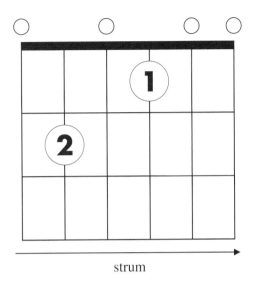

strum

Likewise, A7 is easier than A.

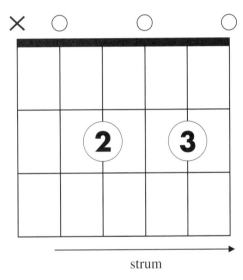

strum

Seventh chords like these are used all the time in bluesy or funky songs.

IT'S YOUR THING

Words and Music by
Rudolph Isley, Ronald Isley and O'Kelly Isley

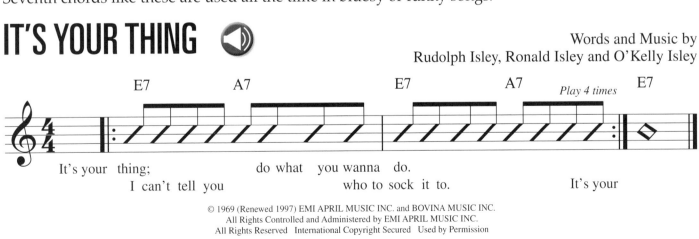

It's your thing;
I can't tell you
do what you wanna do.
who to sock it to.
It's your

TEACHER MELODY:

etc.

ROCK AROUND THE CLOCK

Words and Music by
Max C. Freedman and Jimmy DeKnight

Intro

One, two, three o'clock, four o'clock rock. Five, six, seven o'clock, eight o'clock rock.

Nine, ten, eleven o'clock, twelve o'clock rock. We're gonna rock around the clock tonight. Put your

Verse

glad rags on and join me hon. We'll have some fun when the

Chorus

clock strikes one. We're gonna rock around the clock tonight. We're gonna

rock, rock, rock, 'til the broad daylight. We're gonna

rock, gonna rock around the clock tonight.

TEACHER MELODY:

THE FULL G7 CHORD

Here's the full, six-string version of the G7 chord you learned in Book 1.

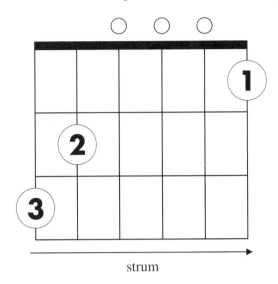

strum

GIVE ME ONE REASON

Words and Music
by Tracy Chapman

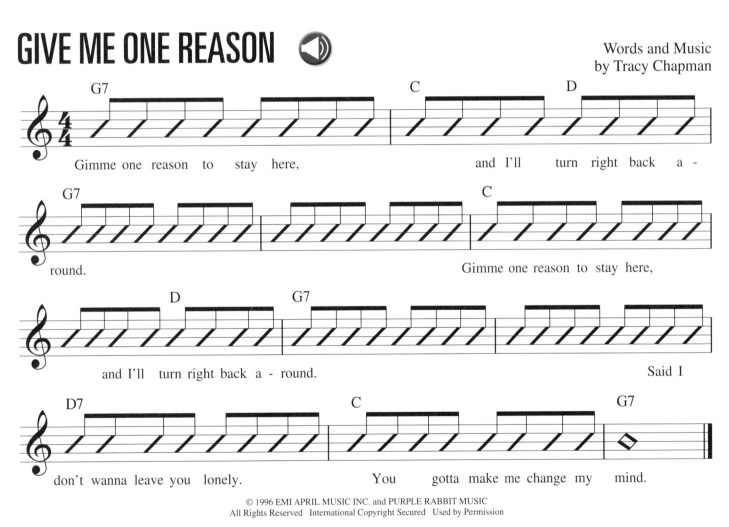

G7

Gimme one reason to stay here,

C   D

and I'll turn right back a -

G7

round.

C

Gimme one reason to stay here,

D   G7

and I'll turn right back a - round.

Said I

D7

don't wanna leave you lonely.

C

You gotta make me change my

G7

mind.

TEACHER MELODY:

G7   C   D7   G7

etc.

THE NOTES D, E & F

Let's check out the notes on the 4th string. For the note D, pluck the open 4th string.

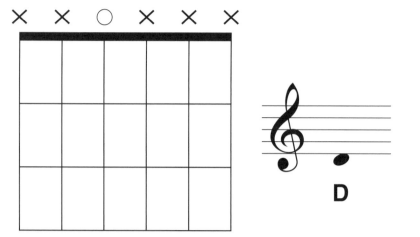

For the note E, use your 2nd finger to press the 4th string at the 2nd fret.

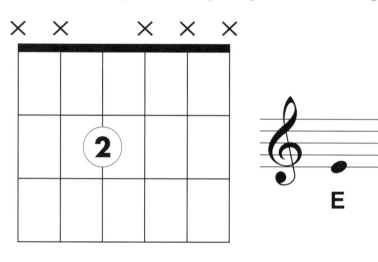

For the note F, use your 3rd finger to press the 4th string at the 3rd fret.

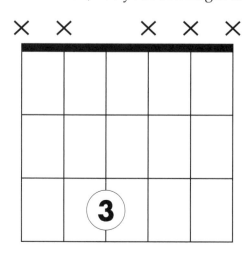

TWO-STRING ROCK

Count: 1 and (2) and 3 and (4) and 1 and (2) and 3 4

TEACHER ACCOMPANIMENT:

GREEN ONIONS

Written by Al Jackson, Jr., Lewis Steinberg,
Booker T. Jones and Steve Cropper

TEACHER ACCOMPANIMENT:

THE C MAJOR SCALE

A **scale** is a collection of notes used to make melodies and chords. You now know enough notes to play a C major scale.

STAIR STEPPING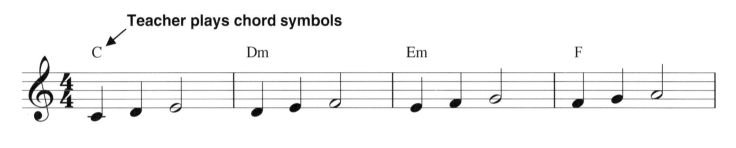

RINGING BELLS

TEACHER ACCOMPANIMENT:

THE NOTES C♯ & F♯

You've now learned notes on each string. But there are other notes in between the ones you've learned as well. Let's learn a few of these right now. The ♯ symbol is called a **sharp**. So these notes are read as "C sharp" and "F sharp."

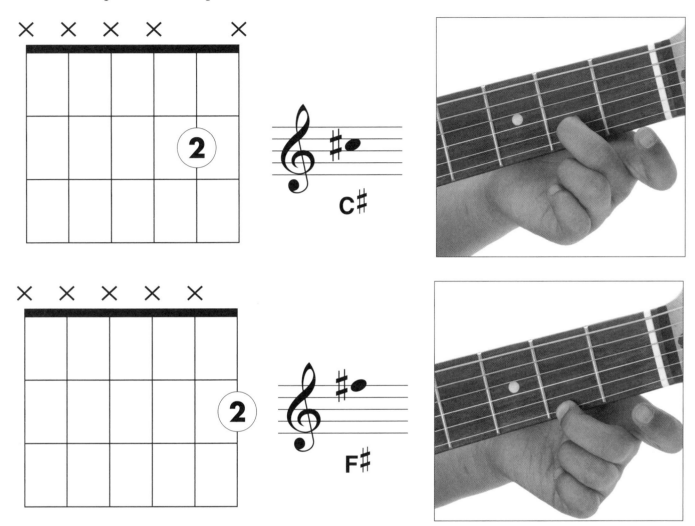

C♯

F♯

THAT SOUNDS SHARP!

TEACHER ACCOMPANIMENT:

let ring throughout

POWER CHORDS

So far, you've learned major, minor, and seventh chords, but there's another kind of chord called a **power chord**. These have only two different notes in them, and they sound great in rock songs. Try these out on an electric guitar if you have one!

THE E5 CHORD

Use your 1st finger to press the 5th string at the 2nd fret. Strum only the 6th and 5th strings.

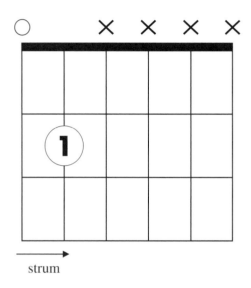

ONE-CHORD ROCK

TEACHER ACCOMPANIMENT:

THE A5 & D5 CHORDS

This is just like the E5 chord, only we move over one string.

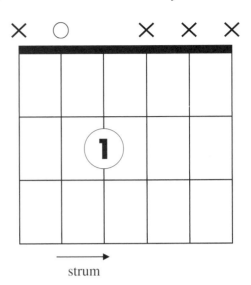

strum

And we move over one more string for the D5 chord.

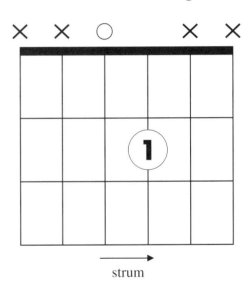

strum

OYE COMO VA

Words and Music by Tito Puente

Oye como va,   mi ritmo.   Bueno 'pa gozar   mulata.

TEACHER MELODY:

THE B MINOR CHORD

Here's one more new chord to learn before we play the final song.

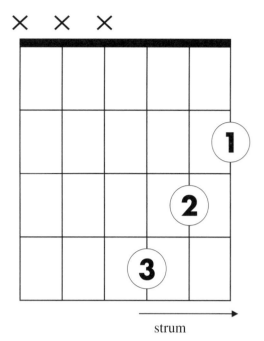

× × ×

① ② ③

strum

Great job! For this final song, you know enough to play either the chords or the melody!

EIGHT DAYS A WEEK 🔊

Words and Music by
John Lennon and Paul McCartney

Verse

D   E   G   D

Ooh, I need your love, babe. Guess you know it's true.

E   G   D

Hope you need my love, babe, just like I need you.

Chorus

Bm   G   Bm   E

Hold me, love me. Hold me, love me.

CERTIFICATE OF ACHIEVEMENT

Congratulations to

_____

(YOUR NAME)

_____

(DATE)

You have completed

GUITAR FOR KIDS BOOK 2

_____

(TEACHER SIGNATURE)

You are now ready for

HAL LEONARD GUITAR METHOD BOOK 1